Ook the Book

by Lissa Rovetch

illustrated by
Shannon McNeill

chronicle books · san francisco

I am **Ook,**
Ook the **book.**
Do you see me
in my **nook?**
Will you stop
and take a **look?**
You will see,
I'm one good **book!**

I am **Ake,**

Ake the **snake.**

I can **bake.** See my **cake?**

If you **take** my **snake cake,**

I will put you in the **lake!**

In the twin

I am In, In the twin.
I am as thin as a pin!

My pig, Lin
is not so thin.

Ug the Bug

I am Ug,
Ug the bug.

This is Glug,
Glug the slug.

Do you want a **bug slug hug?**

I am **At**,
At the **cat**.

Do you see **Pat?**
He is my **rat**.

I sat on **Pat**,
so he is **flat**.

I am **Et**,
Et the **pet**.
Et the **wet pet** in a **net**.
Do you need a **wet net pet?**
You can **get**
me free I **bet**.

Ee the Bee

I am Ee,
Ee the bee.

Do you see Lee,
up in the tree?

You are **free** to look for **Lee.**

But **gee**, that **bee** is hard to **see!**

Eep the Sheep

I am **Eep**,
Eep the **sheep**.
This is **Peep**.
She needs to **sleep**.
Please do not
make that **jeep**

go **beep!**

Io the Kid

I am Id, Id the kid.

Did you see what I just did?

I hid a squid under old Sid!

I am Ing,

Ing the thing.

I bring string

to the king.

If you need

a bit of string,

just give a ring,

to Ing the thing.

Ow the Cow

I am **Ow**,
Ow the **cow**.
I can bark. **Bow wow wow**.
Don't ask me why,
don't ask me **how**.
I am just that kind
of **cow**.

THE FLY

I am **Y**, **Y** the **fly**. It is time to say goodbye.

I will **try** not to **cry**.

But **my**, it's hard to say goodbye!

pet

Net

wet.

cow

bow wow wow

squid

Look

book

Nook

Glug

hug

cat

Lin

pin

twin